SALARY MANAGEMENT

SALARY MANAGEMENT

by Derek Coulthard

The Industrial Society

First published 1971 by
The Industrial Society
Peter Runge House
3 Carlton House Terrace
London SW1Y 5DG
Telephone 01–839 4300

Revised 1975, 1979, 1983
Second edition 1989
© *The Industrial Society, 1971, 1989*

ISBN 0 85290 415 0

British Library Cataloguing in Publication Data:
Coulthard, Derek
    Salary management – 3rd ed.
    1. Remuneration. Management aspects
    I. Title   II. Industrial Society   III. Series
    658.3'2

Typeset by Columns of Reading
Printed and bound in Great Britain by Belmont Press, Northampton

CONTENTS

FOREWORD

Whatever the discipline or level of management, the responsibilities of a manager are many and various. It is their job to produce results with essentially just two resources— people and time.

To maximise the potential of both, most managers need some reminders and basic guidelines to help them.

The Notes for Managers series provides succinct yet comprehensive coverage of key management issues and skills. The short time it takes to read each title will pay dividends in terms of utilising one of those key resources— people.

ALISTAIR GRAHAM
Director, The Industrial Society

I

SALARY MANAGEMENT

Introduction

Small organisations usually have an informal salary structure which reflects the flexible approach required in a growing business. However, when expansion takes place and employee numbers begin to grow over 50 then it is time to adopt a more formal approach.

This booklet describes how to go about establishing a salary structure for staff grades based on sound and well-tried principles.

Objectives of a salary policy

In overall terms the aim of a formal salary policy is to ensure that employees are paid in accordance with the value to the company of the work they perform. This aim should be incorporated into the salary policy which should be tailor-made to meet the needs and objectives of the organisation as a whole. An example of a salary policy is given in Appendix 1.

Responsibility for salary management

The responsibility for sound salary management lies with line management. In small organisations the senior line manager or director will have overall responsibility for the policy but in larger firms the detailed aspects of salary administration will be co-ordinated by the personnel officer.

It is very important that all members of line management understand the aims and content of the salary policy because it is their responsibility to explain it to staff and operate it correctly within their own departments.

Communicating salary policy

Equally important as the preparation of a salary policy is the need to communicate it to everyone concerned; indeed there is no reason why every staff member should not have a copy of the actual policy.

By far the best way of passing on information is for departmental managers to call a briefing meeting with all their staff to explain in general terms what the policy covers and how it will operate. Care should be taken to ensure that each employee's questions are answered sympathetically and honestly without going into detail on individual cases.

A successful briefing session will dispel fears. Failure to do so will result in the grapevine taking over with often disastrous consequences.

Job description

Every organisation has both formal and informal aspects regarding who reports to whom and how work is done. When developing a salary policy, however, it is necessary to have a clear picture of the content of jobs and the formal reporting arrangements. This is not a difficult exercise and in most small organisations can be completed in a few months. Job descriptions are easy to complete and invaluable because they have many uses. For example, they can be used for job evaluation, on-job training, appraisal of staff, and, of course, recruitment.

A job description is a basic statement covering such items as:

- job title
- department
- to whom responsible

- job titles of subordinates
- overall purpose of the job
- duties and responsibilities
- limits of authority.

Furthermore, don't forget the *date of preparation*.

The completed job description must be agreed by both the job holder and relevant supervisor. A short, punchy style of writing should be adopted and the golden rule is to keep it short and simple.

An example of a job description is given in Appendix 2.

Job evaluation

Many organisations avoid introducing job evaluation because they feel it is either too costly or too sophisticated. This need not be the case. Two methods can be considered as practicable:

1 ranking
2 classification.

Ranking

Ranking involves studying all the job descriptions and placing them in order of importance. Note that it is the job which is being evaluated and not the person doing it. Here is a 'plan of attack'.

- Set up a committee of, say, three people who have a good knowledge of all the jobs being covered.
- Select about 15–20 jobs as being a good representative sample of all the jobs being covered. These are the benchmarks or key jobs and form the basis of job evaluation.
- Write job descriptions for these key jobs.
- Separately rank these jobs and seek agreement with other

committee members.

- Design a job questionnaire (see Appendix 3).
- Brief all employees on the value of well-written job descriptions and explain how they should complete them (see Appendix 4).
- Ensure that all descriptions are agreed by the respective supervisors.
- Call the committee together to slot in the jobs according to the benchmarks to reach an overall rank order.

An extension of ranking known as 'paired' or 'forced' comparisons should be considered. Each job is compared with every other job and a decision made as to which job is the more important. It is rather like filling in a football coupon.

If the job is more important, insert 2; if equally important, insert 1; if less important, insert 0. For example, in this chart an accounts clerk is considered less important than a receptionist and more important than a messenger.

An example of paired or forced comparisons

	A	B	C	D	E	F	G	H	J	K
Accounts clerk (A)	x	1	0	0	2	0	0	0	1	0
Invoice typist (B)	1	x	0	0	2	0	0	0	1	0
Receptionist/telephonist (C)	2	2	x	1	2	1	0	1	2	1
Wages clerk (D)	2	2	1	x	2	1	0	1	2	2
Messenger (E)	0	0	0	0	x	0	0	0	0	0
Costing clerk (F)	2	2	1	1	2	x	0	1	2	1
Director's secretary (G)	2	2	2	2	2	2	x	2	2	2
Shorthand-typist (H)	2	2	1	1	2	1	0	x	2	1
Stock clerk (J)	1	1	0	0	2	0	0	0	x	0
Sales clerk (K)	2	2	1	1	2	1	0	1	1	x

(An 'x' is entered where a job is being compared with itself.)

Reading from the left, compare each job in turn with every other job shown along the top (signified here by initial letters).

Once this is done, a matrix is drawn up showing the jobs in rank order, for example:

Rank order following paired or forced comparisons

Director's secretary	2	2	2	2	2	2	2	2	2
Receptionist/telephonist		2	2	2	2	1	1	1	1
Wages clerk		2	2	2	2	1	1	1	1
Costing clerk		2	2	2	2	1	1	1	1
Shorthand-typist		2	2	2	2	1	1	1	1
Sales clerk		2	2	2	1	1	1	1	1
Invoice typist							2	1	1
Stock clerk							2	1	1
Accounts clerk							2	1	1
Messenger									0

A word of warning: thirty is the maximum number of jobs which can be ranked manually, so do not attempt to include more than this number.

Job classification

Job classification is, like ranking, a non analytical method of job evaluation. It is a method of separating jobs into natural groups according to a pre-determined classification system. For an example, *see* Appendix 5. To develop your own classification scheme you will need to:

1 rank 15–20 benchmark jobs
2 decide natural breakpoints between groups of jobs

3 define in words the common features which the jobs in a particular group share
4 rank a further 15–20 and slot them in with the first group
5 refine the wording used for each classification as necessary.

The advantages of this method are:

- quick and simple to operate
- can be reasonably defended in an appeal situation
- can cover a large number of jobs.

The disadvantages of this method are:

- not suitable when jobs have a complex skill content and range
- has a limited life of about four years.

Operating the scheme

Job descriptions are written task-by-task. Each task is allotted a grading by matching the task descriptions with the grade description. When grading is completed, the number of grades accorded is totted up and a decision made by the committee on the overall grading, for example:

Grade	A	B	C	D	E
Number of tasks allocated to grades	2	8	3	–	–

The decision is made on a whole job basis as to whether the job is, say an A, B or C grade job. Some schemes allow for an approximate percentage of the job holders' time spent on each task as the determining feature, but on this basis it is terribly easy to add 2 and 2 to get 5!

Drawing up grades

Whether the ranking method or the classification method of job evaluation is used, the aim is to arrive at groups of jobs or grades containing broadly similar-sized jobs.

In general, jobs will tend to fall into broad groups, but there are bound to be a few jobs which will cause some soul-searching. The grading completed, the jobs on either side of the grade must be scrutinised carefully to ensure they are in the right group. In the event of appeals being raised it is likely that they will spring from this grey area.

Five grades ought to suffice, up to and including supervisory level. To have more will mean that differentials between grades will be narrowed and staff will see little financial advantage in taking on more responsibility. In addition, the personnel officer may be faced with an excessive number of requests for upgrading each time there is a slight increase in responsibility or change in job content.

Analysing the results of job evaluation

Once the job evaluation has been completed and the jobs have been grouped into grades it is time to think about salaries. The use of graphs is invaluable at this stage when creating a new salary structure. By presenting the infor-mation visually, anomalies will stand out and a clearer picture will emerge of the current position.

As an aid to determining the new salary structure it is very helpful to create a scattergram. An example is given in Appendix 6, but here is how it is done.

1 On a graph, plot each job holder by basic salary and grade. This will give you the scatter on your current salary structure.
2 Draw a curved line through the centre of the scatter so that there are roughly the same number of points above as below the line. This 'line of best fit', as it is called, will

illustrate your salary practice now. It represents the current mid-points of each of the new grades.

3 Salary ranges can now be added with the maximum and minimum salary levels drawn between 12% and 25% above and below the lines. Jobs falling above the maximum and below the minimum are, of course, anomalies in the new structure. Appendix 7 shows a typical salary structure.

We now have a formal salary structure based on job evaluation which reflects accurately the current organisation structure. The next step is to decide how this matches up against the outside market for a similar range of jobs.

Surveying the outside market

There are a number of ways of finding out how your current salaries compare with the external market.

- By purchasing professional salary surveys such as those published by Reward Regional Surveys or the Institute of Administrative Management. Both these organisations can provide information on up-to-date salary trends in any part of the country.
- By telephoning your opposite number in other organisations in the area and exchanging information.
- By sending to selected organisations a job description from each grade and asking for a comparison. (It is wise to telephone personally to enquire if the organisation is willing to take part.) This must be followed up by sending to the participants details of the survey but excluding actual organisation names.
- By inviting four or five opposite numbers in your area to form a Pay Policy Comparison Club with the first meeting on your premises. An agreed agenda should be drawn up stating jobs to be discussed in order that salary and benefits information is forthcoming.

When considering salary survey information, care must be taken to ensure that as far as possible you are comparing like with like. Some salary surveys rely heavily on job titles when gathering their data and it is well-known that different organisations often pay very different salaries to jobs with the same title.

On balance, using selected job descriptions and gathering information on these from other local organisations is the most reliable method of obtaining salary data for your location.

Deciding final salary structure

So far we have:

- Established a grading structure and allocated all the jobs to a grade using sound job evaluation methods.
- Established what our current salary practice line is and added maximum and minimum salary levels for each grade (see Appendix 6).
- Surveyed the external market place and gathered information on how we measure up in terms of market rates.

If the salary survey data indicate that your salary rates are low compared to rates paid by other similar organisations, consideration should be given to adjusting your salary ranges to ensure you are competitive. You may, for example, decide to adjust your salary ranges so that the mid-point of each range is equivalent to the market median (defined as the point in a range of values at which 50% of the sample is higher and 50% is lower). Cost considerations will, of course, be a major factor in deciding your new salary structure and thorough costing of proposals must be carried out first.

As a general rule, organisations which pay their staff at the lower quartile level (defined as the point at which 25% of the sample is lower and 75% higher) may experience difficulty in recruiting and retaining good quality staff. The cost of moving salary ranges up to match market rates must be balanced with the high cost of labour turnover which is often a result of low pay. Appendix 8 shows an example of the final salary structure.

Salary anomalies

Once salary ranges have been finalised it will be found that the majority of staff will be on a salary within the new grade boundaries. However, there may be a number of staff who are either over- or under-paid. Those under-paid should be brought up to at least the minimum for the grade. Apart from explaining the situation to those staff who are over the maximum for their job grade, the following should be considered:

- promotion to higher grade work
- rearrangement of job content in order that some higher-grade work is included
- salary standstill until the new maximum overtakes the individual's current rate.

Rate-for-age

Some organisations find it useful to retain a rate-for-age scale to enable young employees to progress on a formal basis as they gain work experience. Rate-for-age reviews can be made quarterly or six monthly and combined with a full review of progress in the job. It is preferable to ensure that young adults are paid at least the minimum of the grade applicable to their job by their eighteenth birthday.

Employee benefits

It is worthwhile mentioning that, when constructing a new salary structure, consideration must be given to the adequacy of existing employee benefits. When conducting a salary survey, employee benefits must also be taken into account.

While staff accept employee benefits as a fact of life, different social groups within the organisation and, indeed, within the area, will view different benefits with varying degrees of interest. Young people are more attracted to an organisation by the promise of a realistic salary than the offer of a generous sick pay or pension scheme. Assisted house purchase, membership of a hospital scheme and share option schemes are likely to appeal to management.

In designing the salary structure, therefore, it is important to consider how much influence employee benefits have on the *total* salary package, i.e. the *real* cost of employing staff.

Performance appraisal

Performance appraisal is a two-way exchange of information between boss and subordinate about the job and the job holder's performance. It provides valuable information on the employee's training and development needs and assists in assessing potential for future jobs. It is also an essential method of reviewing an employee's concerns and aspirations as well as jointly deciding priorities and targets for the future.

More and more organisations today are linking pay directly to achievement and abandoning systems whereby everyone receives the same salary review regardless of performance.

One method of differentially rewarding employees is to place their overall performance in the job into one of five performance categories.

Great care should be exercised to ensure that all managers and supervisors responsible for appraising the performance of their staff are being consistent in their interpretation of the performance categories. Several meetings will need to be held before and after the appraisal discussions to ensure that a consistent and equitable approach has been adopted. It is likely that the majority of employees will be in the 'effective' category with only relatively few who are above and below the standard performance level.

Once the classification of performance has taken place, differential salary awards can be made to those in each category. Whereas it may be appropriate to give a 5% increase to those in the effective category, employees whose performance is classed as superior might receive a 7% increase. Careful costing must be carried out before the final amounts are decided.

How much the organisation can afford to pay will be the overriding consideration when determining the final distribution of amounts.

Performance	
Category	Definition
Unsatisfactory	The employee has not performed to the minimum standard required in the job.
Incomplete	The employee has performed well in most areas of the job but there are areas which need substantial improvement. (This category can also be used for those who have not been in the job very long and who have some way to go before becoming fully proficient in all aspects.)
Effective	The job holder has reached and maintained the level of performance required by the organisation. This is experienced worker standard. All tasks and objectives have been achieved.
Superior	The employee has exceeded the standard level of performance required. There will be significant achievement of results in areas beyond the basic requirements of the job.
Exceptional	The job holder's performance is such that outstanding results have been achieved in the most important aspects of the job. All targets have been exceeded.

Departmental budgets

Every department should have a budget and, within this, there should be an agreed figure for salaries. This should be decided one year in advance and should take into consideration staffing requirements, promotions and increases in staff complement. The budget should also take into account a figure to be set aside for salary increases. This can either be an agreed lump sum or, more usually, a percentage of the departmental salary budget.

Salary review procedures

It is usual in most organisations for staff to have an annual review of salary except for trainees and those under 18 years of age who may receive more regular reviews.

Salary reviews should be carefully planned with adequate briefing of managers and supervisors on the guidelines for the review, the timing, and the communication of the results to staff.

Documentation will be required on which managers can make their salary recommendations (see Appendix 9). Once all the recommendations have been made the results should be reviewed to ensure the guidelines have been correctly followed. It is usual for the final figures to be agreed at director level before staff are informed of the results of the review.

Once employees have been advised of their increases, managers must gather feedback on reaction to the review. Not everyone will be happy at the outcome, but if the communication process has been thorough staff should understand the reasons behind the review.

Management salaries

Most of this booklet has been devoted to salaried staff up to supervisory level. However, the same principles apply to management staff, although the type of job evaluation system used for management is often more involved.

And finally . . .

Remember how important the job description is as a management tool. Keeping job descriptions up-to-date is essential because they are the key to many decisions regarding staff. The following diagram illustrates this.

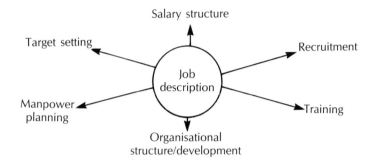

II

APPENDICES

APPENDIX 1

MODEL SALARY POLICY

1 **Introduction**

The aim of this document is to set down the organisation's policy with regard to salary. It is the responsibility of all who apply it to explain it fully to their subordinates.

2 **Aims**

The aims of the organisation's policy are:

- to recognise the value of all jobs relative to each other within the organisation and in comparison with similar jobs outside
- to recognise the value of the individual to the organisation and to relate this to the salary range applicable to the job.

3 **Salary structure**

The salary structure will be based on job evaluation. Each job will have declared minimum and maximum salary range and it is the organisation's policy to pay at least the minimum for each job.

4 **Job evaluation**

It is the policy of the organisation to ensure that staff are fully involved in job evaluation. Moreover, a staff representative will be a member of the job evaluation committee.

Job evaluation is a continuing process and once salary grades have been established, the team will meet regularly to deal with regrading of existing jobs as well as grading new jobs.

5 **Initial salary**

In determining an individual's salary on appointment, no differentiation is made on the grounds of race, sex or age. In addition, the following features are taken into account:

- the value to the organisation of the relevant experience the individual brings

- the individual's value in the outside market
- the individual's value in comparison to existing staff who hold similar jobs.

6 Performance appraisal

An integral part of salary management is the regular appraisal of staff. This helps to determine training needs and it is the basis upon which management counsels individuals in order that employees have maximum opportunity to develop their own potential. During the appraisal, short- and longer-term targets will be mutually agreed with management for the year ahead.

7 Salary reviews

It is the policy of the organ–sation to review the salaries of all staff on an annual basis. Those under 18 years will be reviewed on a quarterly basis.

8 Promotion

An individual who is promoted to higher-grade work will have a salary increase of 10% or will be paid the minimum for the new grade, whichever is the greater.

If an individual is required by the organisation to take work of a lower grade, there will be no salary decrease. Instead there will be a salary standstill until the rate of the new position equals that of the old.

9 Progression within salary range

Everyone will know the salary range for their job. Those who do their job particularly well will reach the maximum for their salary range within four years.

10 Right of appeal

Anyone who feels unhappy about the application of this policy has the right to appeal first to their manager and then to the Managing Director, whose decision will be final. The individual has a right to bring along a colleague to help his or her appeal.

MODEL JOB DESCRIPTION

JOB TITLE: DATE:
Secretary to Chief Project Engineer

DEPARTMENT: AGREED BY:
Project Engineering   Chief Project Engineer

RESPONSIBLE TO: JOB TITLES OF
Chief Project Engineer   SUBORDINATES:
                        None

OVERALL PURPOSE:
To provide a complete secretarial service to Chief Project Engineer
by organising the routine aspects of the work.

Daily tasks:
1 On receipt of mail, sort into order of priority, attach previous
   correspondence, if any, and type routine letters for signature.
2 Take dictation from Chief Project Engineer and deal with urgent
   correspondence dictated by senior project engineers.
3 Against a timetable, type complicated statistical tables connected with department's project work.
4 Deal with department's travel arrangements and prepare travel itineraries.
5 Maintain simple time records concerning progress of experimental projects. Ensure that progress charts are kept up-to-date
6 Act as an assistant to Chief Project Engineer by dealing with the more routine aspects of the work.
7 Act as 'shield' by dealing with callers personally and on the telephone.

Weekly tasks:
Prepare for accountant short summary of expenses incurred by department during previous week, and allocate to individual projects.

Monthly tasks:
Collect brief reports prepared by senior engineers on their respective projects and type draft of progress report for the Project Engineering Director.

Six monthly tasks:
Transfer old files to basement and make out new files for next six months.

Annually:
Type statement of account showing income over expenditure on previous year's projects.

Job requirements and other information:

Minimum age:	21 years.
Educational qualifications:	5 'O' levels (including English language) and secretarial college training.
Experience:	3 years' practical office experience including 1 year in a similar firm.
Induction:	3 months.
Other information:	The Chief Project Engineer is frequently off-site and the secretary is expected to deal with all routine problems arising during these periods.

APPENDIX 3

MODEL JOB EVALUATION QUESTIONNAIRE

Job title: ....

Department: ....

Responsible to: ....

Agreed by: ....Date: ....

---

1 What is the overall purpose of the job?

---

2 Draw up a family tree showing the job in relation to others in the department.

---

3 Give a concise description of the main areas of responsibility in the job. Take it area-by-area and stress the important features.

Daily tasks:

Weekly tasks:

Monthly tasks:

Quarterly tasks:

Half yearly tasks:

Annual tasks:

---

4 Give the titles of the jobs which you directly supervise.

---

5 Who do you contact inside and outside the organisation during the course of your job? Is contact by telephone or in person? Comment on the reason for contact.

Internal:

External:

---

6 Do you handle confidential information? If so, describe.

_____

7 Comment on the qualifications and/or experience necessary to
do the job effectively.

_____

8 Other information:

_____

APPENDIX 4

MODEL JOB EVALUATION BRIEFING NOTES

Introduction

Job evaluation is a method of looking objectively at jobs and ranking them in order of importance. By comparing them one with another, each job will be placed in a grade relative to its worth. However, it must be stressed that it is the *job* which is being examined and *not* the individual.

A job evaluation committee has been formed under the chairmanship of Andrew Brown, the Company Secretary. The other members of the committee are Alan Green and Jill Black. The job evaluation committee will be responsible for carrying out the job evaluation and grading.

The scheme

After a great deal of investigation, the committee has decided to use a classification scheme, a copy of which is attached. All members of staff will be required to provide full details of their jobs using the attached questionnaire.

Completing the questionnaire

1 Overall purpose

One sentence will normally suffice here. It should be concise and give the reason for the job's existence in order that the committee has 'something to hang its cap on' before looking at the job in depth, e.g.

Process all orders ensuring that departmental computer codes are included and that VAT figure is correct.

2 Family tree

A clearer picture of your job is given if you draw up a family tree of your department showing your job in relation to other jobs.

3 Job description

It is always difficult to write one's own job description: consider therefore that you are transferring to another department in the organisation and that you must prepare a note for your successor covering the elements of the job. Describe the job as it is and not how it should be. (If you feel you are going into too much detail, it probably means that you are just about right!)

Write down the area headings first. For example: correspondence, planning, queries, staff, and describe the responsibility involved under each heading, e.g.

> Correspondence – on receipt of mail, decide what can be delegated to subordinates and retain non-routine letters. Where necessary give instructions regarding the handling of particular letters.

4 Supervisory responsibility

Supervisory responsibility can be assessed fairly only by examining carefully the job description of those jobs under your jurisdiction.

5 Contacts

The strength of the organisation lies in the service given to customers. This does not diminish the value of internal contacts. What is important is the level at which contact is normally made and the reason for contact in the first place.

6 Confidential information

Describe in this section any confidential information which you handle regularly in the job. For example: personnel records, salaries or company plans.

7 Qualifications and/or experience

Comment should be made here regarding the minimum qualifications and/or experience which might be brought to the job before it can be done effectively. It may be possible to state an actual qualification or the job may call for 'an aptitude for figures'. Experience required must be quite specific. For example: six months' practical experience in credit control.

8 Other information

No questionnaire can possibly cover all aspects of a job and since it is important that all staff have the opportunity to comment on all areas of the job which are important to them, space is provided for this, e.g.

> Large proportion of work is concerned with meeting tight time schedules.

These comments should cover features which are an integral part of the job and not temporary difficulties.

Completion date for questionnaires

All questionnaires must be completed and returned to Alan Green by Monday, 29 March.

Completion date for job evaluation exercise
With the co-operation of everyone, the committee hopes to complete the grading exercise by 15 May.

Right of appeal
Any member of staff who feels their job has not been fairly evaluated has the right to appeal to the team through their head of department. They can then expect to be invited, along with the head of department, to discuss the job in detail with the members of the committee. The decision by the committee following the appeal will be final.

APPENDIX 5

EXAMPLE OF JOB CLASSIFICATION SCHEME

Grade A: Tasks are simple and conform to clearly laid down procedures. All written work and calculations are checked. Up to a few weeks' training required.

Grade B: Tasks are subject to laid down procedures but can involve a limited measure of initiative. Work subject to spot checks. Up to six months' training or experience required.

Grade C: Tasks are carried out and decisions made in accordance with standard procedures, subject to infrequent supervision. Routine contact, external and internal, up to own level to obtain and provide information. Probable minimum of two years' experience or training.

Grade D: After specific direction, plans and arranges work within main work programme with little or no supervision. Only non-routine problems referred to supervisor. May have supervisory responsibility. Can have contact at higher level than own, external and internal, to obtain and give information which may be of a confidential nature. Specialised knowledge may be required. Probably five years' experience.

Grade E: After general direction, plans and arranges work with little or no supervision. Tasks can involve work of non-routine nature requiring an original approach as to planning and method. Would normally have contact at higher level than own, external and internal, to obtain and give information which may be of confidential nature. Can be required to make decisions as to daily action and direct work of subordinates. More than five years' experience required.

APPENDIX 6

USING A SCATTERGRAM TO DRAW UP A SALARY STRUCTURE

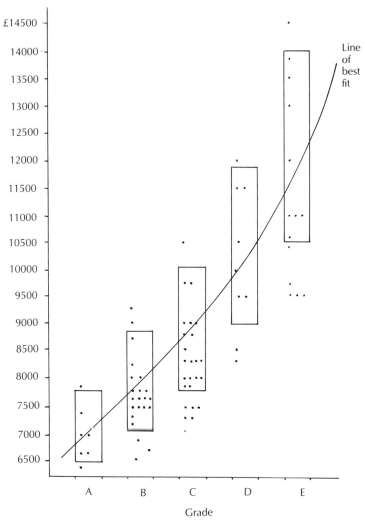

● :Number of people within each grade along with their current salary

APPENDIX 7

SALARY STRUCTURE AFTER A JOB EVALUATION EXERCISE

Grade A £6500–£7850
      B £7200–£8800
      C £7850–£10050
      D £9000–£11750
      E £10400–£14000

Note that the maximum figures for each grade are between 30% and 45% above the minimum figures and the base for the next grade is at approximately the midpoint of the previous grade. The structure is based on the scattergram in Appendix 6.

APPENDIX 8

FINAL SALARY STRUCTURE AFTER ADJUSTMENT TO MATCH MARKET RATES
(5% up on Appendix 7)

Grade A   £6725–£8142
      B   £7460–£9140
      C   £8142–£10452
      D   £9350–£11237
      E   £10820–£14600

APPENDIX 9

SALARY REVIEW FORM

Salary review—1 April 198

CONFIDENTIAL

DEPARTMENT . . . .

1 Name	2 Job title	3 Age at 31/3	4 Service at 31/3	5 Date last perfor- mance increase	6 Amount	7 Present salary	8 Grade	9 Maxi- mum salary	10 Perfor- mance category this year	11 Proposed increase	12 New salary	13 Remark
Total												

FURTHER READING

Garnett, J. *The manager's responsibility for communication*. The Industrial Society, 1989.

Scott, K. *Clerical job grading and merit rating*. Institute of Administrative Management, 1983.

McBeath, G. & Rands, D.N. *Salary administration*. Business Books Ltd, 1976.

Clerical salaries analysis. Annual survey and supplements. Institute of Administrative Management.

Lawson, I. *Appraisal and appraisal interviewing*. The Industrial Society, 1989.

Lawson, I. *Target setting*. The Industrial Society, 1989.

Pearson, S. & Coulthard, D. *Personnel procedures and records*. Gower, 1987.